WHOSE FEET?

by

Rebecca Phillips-Bartlett

Minneapolis, Minnesota

Credits

Images are courtesy of Shutterstock.com. With thanks to Getty Images, Thinkstock Photo, and iStockphoto. Cover – Rashad Ashur, Andi111, Dennis W, Ramligallery. 2–3 – Jurie Maree, Elizabeth Caron. 4–5 – foaloce, JeyArt. 6–7 – Aksenova Natalya, Ekkachai, Krakenimages.com, Olhastock, guntur alfian, GraphicsRF.com. 8–9 – Allexxandar, Andrzej Kubik. 10–11 – Elizabeth Caron, Helen J Davies, Matthias Korn, photomaster, Sergey Uryadnikov. 12–13 – hakoar, worldswildlifewonders, brgfx. 14–15 – Dirk Ercken, Kurit afshen, Ramligallery. 16–17 – Kurit afshen, Lauren Suryanata. 18–19 – Eric Isselee, Nailia Schwarz, Pedro Helder Pinheiro, Sergej Razvodovskij. 20–21 – AndyElliott, Sergej Razvodovski, Shawn Levin, wong salam. 22–23 – BOOCYS, CSNafzger, Jurie Maree, KlavdiyaV, Papa Bravo.

Bearport Publishing Company Product Development Team

Publisher: Jen Jenson; Director of Product Development: Spencer Brinker; Managing Editor: Allison Juda; Editor: Cole Nelson; Associate Editor: Naomi Reich; Associate Editor: Tiana Tran; Art Director: Colin O'Dea; Designer: Kim Jones; Designer: Kayla Eggert; Product Development Specialist: Owen Hamlin

Library of Congress Cataloging-in-Publication Data is available at www.loc.gov or upon request from the publisher.

ISBN: 979-8-89232-736-7 (hardcover)
ISBN: 979-8-89232-786-2 (paperback)
ISBN: 979-8-89232-823-4 (ebook)

For more information, write to Bearport Publishing, 5357 Penn Avenue South, Minneapolis, MN 55419.

CONTENTS

WHOSE FEET COULD THESE BE?

Feet help animals **explore** the world around them. But can you guess an animal just from its feet? Who could have left this trail of footprints in the snow?

What can feet tell us about an animal?

On the following pages, you will see photos of some feet and three different animals. Look at the pictures and read the clues to guess whose feet are shown. Then, turn the page to find the answer.

A BIG PAIR OF FEET

Below is the first pair of feet. What do you notice about them?

There are two toes on each foot. This might help the animal run quickly.

These feet look big and strong. Maybe the creature is just as huge.

One toe has a powerful **talon**. Being kicked by that would hurt!

Whose feet could these be? Choose which animal you think best fits the feet.
Ostrich
Emu
Chicken
Those feet are huge! They could crush me!
7

WHOSE FEET ARE THEY?

They are the OSTRICH'S feet!

Who needs to fly? Not me!

Ostriches are the largest birds in the world. Because they are so big, they aren't able to fly. So, ostriches get around by running on their feet.

These big birds have great eyesight. This helps them look out for **predators**. With their fast legs, ostriches can outrun most predators. If running away doesn't work, ostriches will kick. Watch out!

An ostrich's kick is powerful enough to kill a lion!

Ostriches can run more than 40 miles per hour (65 kph).

STRONG, SHARP FEET

Look at those feet on the edge of the rocks! Whose could they be?

This animal has sharp claws on the end of each toe. Could claws help the animal catch **prey**?

Each toe is connected by some skin. This may help the creature swim. They are called webbed feet.

Which of these animals might have feet like these? Pick one.

WHOSE FEET ARE THEY?

They are the **SEA OTTER'S** feet!

Are you talking about me?

Sea otters are **mammals** that live in the water. Their webbed feet almost look like flippers. They use them to swim through their watery homes.

A group of sleeping sea otters is called a raft. Otters in a raft often hold hands or tie themselves together using **kelp**. This keeps the animals from drifting away from one another as they rest.

STICKY, GREEN FEET

There are lots of green plants and leaves in the forest. Can you spot the foot among the greens?

This foot is padded. It is also covered with tiny hairs.

It looks like the animal's foot is green. This could help **camouflage** the creature.

Whose feet are these?
Here are three animals
to choose from.
Gecko
Iguana
Tree frog
I live among
the leaves!

WHOSE FEET ARE THEY?

They are the **GECKO'S** feet!

Did you get it right?

Thanks to the tiny hairs on their feet, geckos are amazing climbers. The hairs help them hold onto trees in their wild homes.

The tiny hairs on a gecko's feet are called setae (SET-ay).

Hair isn't the only thing that helps geckos climb. Their tails do, too! Geckos use them to keep themselves from taking a nasty fall.

If a gecko is caught by a predator, it can drop its tail to escape.

Some kinds of geckos have small claws on their feet.

PADDED FEET

Here is another animal's foot. What can its shape tell us?

This padded foot looks very big! Could it help the animal sneak up on its prey?

It looks like the creature's fur is a golden color.

This foot looks like it could be from a member of the cat family.

Whose padded foot could this be? Make a choice from the following animals.
I have to be super sneaky so my dinner doesn't hear me coming!
Bobcat
Lion
Jaguar

WHOSE FEET ARE THEY?

They are the **LION'S** feet!

Let me sharpen my claws. It's time to catch dinner!

Lion claws work in a way similar to most cats. This large animal can tuck its claws inside its fur. The claws come back out when it's time to hunt.

Lions sometimes use their claws to climb trees.

A lion has five toes on its front paws. The fifth toe is farther back than the rest. It helps the lion hold onto and eat its prey.

BONUS FEET

A rhino's big feet are covered by heavy hooves. Hooves are hard shells that protect an animal's feet. This helps the rhino walk on uneven ground.

HEAVY FEET!

Hooves are made of a **protein** called keratin (KAIR-uh-tin). It is the same thing human fingernails are made of!

WE LOVE TO MEET FANCY FEET!

There are so many kinds of animal feet, from padded to sticky. These feet help creatures climb things, find food, and learn about their world. How do your feet help you?

GLOSSARY

camouflage to hide by blending into the surroundings

explore to search in order to discover something new

kelp a type of seaweed that is long and flat

mammals animals that have hair or fur and drink milk from their mothers as babies

predators animals that hunt other animals for food

prey animals that are eaten by other animals

protein a substance found in all living plants and animals

talon a sharp claw

INDEX